RETURN TO
JERUSALEM

Photography and text by
DAVID GIBBON

Produced by
TED SMART

COLOUR LIBRARY INTERNATIONAL LTD

To my wife Maureen

First published in Great Britain 1977 by Colour Library International Ltd,
80-82, Coombe Road, New Malden, Surrey, England.

Designed by David Gibbon CLI. *Produced by* Ted Smart CLI.
© *Text:* David Gibbon CLI. ©*Illustrations:* David Gibbon CLI.

Printed by INGRA Trento, Italy, and Bound by L.E.G.O. Vicenza, Italy.

Display and Text filmsetting by Focus Photoset, London, England.

ISBN 0 904681 31 9

COLOUR LIBRARY INTERNATIONAL

At my feet the Mount of Olives dropped gently down to the Valley of Kidron and up the far side to where the old city of Jerusalem shimmered in the clear air of the early morning, and the great golden sphere of the Dome of the Rock seemed almost like another sun, setting in the Temple area. Beyond and to the right, hemmed in on all sides by the streets and buildings of the old city and overshadowed by towers and minarets, were the squat cupolas of the Church of the Holy Sepulchre, not easy to make out unless you knew exactly where to look. To the left of the Dome of the Rock, and out of sight, Jews would be swaying and bobbing as they prayed at the Wailing Wall, perhaps pushing written requests and prayers into the spaces between the great stones; the same stones that had mutely witnessed so much of Jerusalem's history, the same stones that had seen, in 70 AD, the destruction of the city by the Roman legions of Titus. It is said that these stones that now comprise the Western Wall were deliberately left intact by Titus as evidence of the power of the Romans; to show future generations, and the world, that their might was such that even cities built of stones of this magnitude had succumbed.

In the narrow arched streets of the old city the Fransiscans—the guardians of the Holy Places, in their brown habits—and the Greek Orthodox in black would, I knew, be going about their business, hurrying through the alleys and the steeply stepped streets, disappearing into, and appearing from, mysterious looking doors in walls. The tea vendors, with their beautifully fashioned and polished tea urns strapped on their backs, and glasses fitted around their waists like cartridges in a gun belt, would be dispensing their hot refreshing drinks. Everywhere guides would be assembling their parties ready to lead them around the confusion that is Jerusalem.

Just below me, so close that I felt I could almost reach out and touch them, were the unmistakable onion shaped domes of the Russian Church of St. Mary Magdalene with its secretive air; great iron gates almost always securely locked. At the foot of the Mount of Olives the Gethsemane Church of all Nations, in my opinion the most beautiful church in Jerusalem, faced straight across the valley to the Golden Gate of the city itself.

I had walked up to this vantage point in the garden of the Dominus Flevit Church, at a very early hour on my first morning back in Jerusalem for two reasons; one was for the lovely view overlooking the whole of the old city and the second was that it allowed me an opportunity to collect my thoughts.

஬ ஬ ஬ ஬ ஬

I think it is very important, before becoming immersed in the facts, the history, the everyday life and all the smaller fascinations that go to make up a city of such complexity as Jerusalem, to step back mentally from it and attempt to view it objectively. If we succeed in doing this we immediately become aware of one major point of great significance that sets Jerusalem apart from all other cities in the world. It is not because it is a grand or particularly beautiful city, for it is not. It is doubtful if any other place on earth can have been more revered, reviled, destroyed, rebuilt and built over than Jerusalem, and it shows. It is not just that here in the city and its surrounding area the scenes were enacted that were to prove to be the foundation of Christianity; nor is it only because Solomon's Temple was built here on Mount Moriah, at the express command of his father David, over the rock upon which it is believed that Abraham was prepared to sacrifice his son Isaac, making the Temple the holiest of holies to all Judaism; nor even because, according to the Muslim faith, it was from this same rock that the prophet Mohammed began his celestial journey. What is astonishing is that these events and all the many others that are associated with them should have taken place here, in an unremarkable and obscure setting in the wilderness, where no rivers meet and there is no port to make the growth of a city likely. It seems that from its inception Jerusalem was intended as the embodiment of an ideal, a sacred rallying point to unite the tribes of Israel and, despite all the wrongs that human beings have been able to accomplish through the centuries, often in the name of the ideals they represented, it is still as an ideal that it exists today.

It was with these thoughts of the ideal of Jerusalem – unity – in mind that I walked down the narrow road that winds past the high walls surrounding the church of St. Mary Magdalene on the right and the back of the Church of All Nations on the left, to come out eventually on the Jericho Road. On the Mount of Olives and down in the Valley of Kidron and up the farther slope, to the very walls of Jerusalem and the Golden Gate lay Jewish, Moslem and Christian cemeteries. It has long been the belief that the final day of judgement will take place here and that to be buried within sight of the Holy City almost guarantees acceptance into heaven. It seemed ironic that here, at least, in death, there was unity.

Just before reaching the Jericho road I could see, on the left, masses of Bougainvillea blossom cascading over the walls surrounding the Garden of Gethsemane. The Garden is one of those places that I find almost impossible to pass without visiting. A quite small doorway set in the wall of the garden allows entry to a paved area with the wall of the church on the left and wrought iron railings on the right separating the paved area from the garden itself. In the garden there are eight ancient olive trees. Although Titus, when he took Jerusalem in 70AD, is said to have cut down all the trees in the area for his war machines, it may be that these particular trees escaped. If not, then new shoots would almost certainly have grown from the roots, for it is said that the olive tree never dies. Botanists have examined these particular specimens and agree that they are very old indeed and some have said that their age might well be as great as two thousand years or more. Whatever the facts of the trees' age, the garden is movingly beautiful and peaceful, tended with loving care, as are all the holy places in the custody of the Franciscans. Understandably, visitors are not normally allowed into the gardens as it would be very easy for irreparable damage to be caused to such a treasured natural site.

The purpose of the Church of All Nations is, of course, to commemorate the agony of Jesus in the Garden before he was betrayed. In the same way as in the Dome of the Rock, therefore, the central point of the church is the large rock over which it is built and which rises up through the floor of the presbytery. Translucent alabaster windows allow a dim and very beautiful light to enter which suffuses the whole church in a soft glow. The present church, the site of which dates back to that originally built at the time of Theodosius in about 380AD, was finished in 1924. As the building of the church was accomplished by financial help from all over the world it was appropriate that it should be given the name of The Church of All Nations. In contrast to the Church of the Holy Sepulchre, the Church of All Nations is utterly peaceful, simple and beautiful. Because the church is in the sole custody of the Franciscans it is possible to ensure that no touts, street vendors or unofficial guides are allowed into either the Garden itself or the church. All over Jerusalem souvenir shops offer a multitude of articles made of olive wood, almost all of which supposedly comes from the Mount of Olives. The same is the case with rosaries said to be made from the seeds of olives from the Garden of Gethsemane. Whatever the truth or otherwise of these claims it is true to say that the fortunate few who are given a rosary by the Franciscans themselves are the owners of some-thing rare, for they collect the olives from the Garden and from the stones they fashion rosaries which are treasured as almost priceless by the lucky recipients.

☖ ☖ ☖ ☖ ☖

In front of me the walls of Jerusalem loomed suddenly massive as, leaving Gethsemane behind me, I climbed up the steep hill that leads to the Lions Gate. These walls, which are very much taken for granted, so much of the life of the city have they become, are a tremendously impressive and beautiful aspect of the city. They are not, of course, the original city walls. They, and the seven gates which give access to the city, date, as does the Tower of David, from the reign of Suleiman the Magnificent, who caused much of the then decaying city to be restored or rebuilt and who was also responsible for the magnificent work on the exterior walls of the Dome of the Rock, including the windows. The actual position and extent of the walls, however, does, in part at least, date from those of Solomon, Herod the Great and Herod Agrippa, although what was the southern part of the city in ancient times, including the original City of David and Mount Zion, is now outside the city walls and Calvary, once outside, is now well within the city. Arguments about the walls and about which site was inside or outside at various times have now been largely resolved by archaeological excavation but, because of the complexities involved I felt it would be helpful to include a map (neither to scale nor exact) that gives some idea of which walls existed at what time in the city's history.

Leaving Divine inspiration and instruction to one side, it is interesting to consider the factors that led to the foundation of Israel and, in particular, to the making of Jerusalem into the capital city, both actual and spiritual, of the Jewish people. Following the Exodus from Egypt, the date of which is difficult to determine but which probably took place between 1400 and 1500 BC, the twelve tribes of Israel, united in the worship of Yahweh, settled in Palestine. The Promised Land was shared amongst the twelve tribes and petty squabbles and jealousies became magnified to the extent that the tribes became truly divided and therefore easy prey to invaders. When this happened the tribes, briefly reunited by a common cause, were able to defeat the enemy. A period of peace followed, as did the renewal of old enmities between the tribes until, once more divided, they again fell prey to enemies from outside. The cycle was repeated again and again until it gradually became clear that, united in the service of their God, the tribes were a match for any foe; divided, and neglecting their God, they were not and they must indeed have felt, with justification, that they were a people chosen to be one nation under God's direction and inspiration.

The story is not an isolated one, we see it time and time again throughout history in various peoples all over the world.

The origins of Uru Salem, the city of Salem, or Jerusalem as we know it today, are lost in the mists of antiquity. Certainly there was a city or settlement on the site in the time of David, for we know that it was to his forces that Jerusalem succumbed, after which, as Lord of Jerusalem, David built a palace on Mount Zion and organized the defences of his new capital. It fell to David's son Solomon, however, to take up the task of levelling the top of Mount Moriah and building the original temple and erecting the first real city walls, and it was under Solomon that Jerusalem achieved the peak of its splendour. Sadly, from almost this time onward, the story of Jerusalem is one of continuing tragedy. That the city has survived at all, in any form, is something of a miracle and an enormous tribute to man's tenacity and his determination to keep alive, at whatever cost, an ideal.

The city of Jerusalem is built on two elongated hills. It stands seven hundred and fifty metres above sea level and one thousand one hundred and fifty metres above the level of the nearby Dead Sea. Divisions within the city are strictly according to faith; the Christian Quarter is situated in the north-west, the Muslim Quarter in the north-east, the Jewish Quarter in the south-east and the Armenian Quarter in the south-west.

The Temple Area, the Haram esh-Sharif (the Enclosure of the Noble Sanctuary) occupies an area of about a hundred and forty four thousand square metres, approximately one sixth of the area of the whole of the Old City. In addition to its size, this vast paved area, on which stand both the Dome of the Rock and the El Aqsa Mosque, is in complete contrast to the rest of the city, which emphasises yet again that this is a holy place, a place set apart, rather than just another section of the city. Here there are no narrow streets, no market stalls or shops to distract the visitor.

After entering the Old City through the Lions Gate I had walked along the road that becomes, further into the city, the Via Dolorosa – the route that is regarded as being the way that Jesus carried His cross to Calvary. Turning left past the Antonia fortress brought me into the Temple area at its north-west corner. The guard on the entrance looked in my camera bag and after making sure that I had nothing more danger-ous than cameras, lenses and film I was free to wander around in this remarkable place. The Dome of the Rock must be one of the most beautiful and inspiring examples of religious architecture anywhere in the world. Any of the eight flights of steps may be chosen to climb up to the terrace, some twelve feet high, around which are soaring arches called Mawazin, meaning scales, where legend says the scales of justice will be suspended to weigh souls on the day of judgement. In fairness, of course, almost any church, mosque or synagogue would be considerably enhanced by being placed in such a spacious and elegant setting. Nevertheless the Dome of the Rock is very beautiful in its own right. A regular octagon in shape, the lower portion is encased in marble, higher up this gives way to Persian and Turkish tiles adorned with the most elaborate and colourful designs and Arabic scripts. The mosaic windows allow only a dim light to filter through into the interior, not unlike that in the Gethsemane Church of all Nations, and in the same way entirely in keeping with the character and purpose of the building.

The focal point of the interior of the Dome of the Rock, and indeed its sole reason for existence, is the natural rock, the summit of Mount Moriah, which lies in the centre of the floor, or rather rises up through it. It is this rock that formed the holocaust altar of the Temple of Solomon, the same rock upon which Abraham was to have sacrificed his son Isaac, and from which Mohammed is said to have commenced his night journey to heaven.

In 1099 the Crusaders transformed the Dome of the Rock into a Christian place of worship, giving it the name Templum Domini. To the Crusader's credit, and to the surprise of Saladin when he re-captured Jerusalem in 1187, little had been altered apart from erecting an iron screen around the rock itself and placing a golden cross on the top of the dome. The iron screen of the Crusaders remains to this day but, of course, the cross was taken down, to be replaced once more by the crescent of Islam.

Throughout its history, with appalling frequency, events overtook Jerusalem and it suffered in the process. To catalogue all such happenings would be pointless, and certainly repetitious. The following, therefore, is simply a chronological list of some of the more important events, spanning some three thousand years.

c. 1000BC David takes Jerusalem from the Jebusites. It was at about this time that the Temple was built, using cedars imported from the Lebanon.

587BC The city is destroyed by Nebuchadnezzar and the Jews are taken into exile in Babylon.

538BC Cyrus, king of Persia, allows the Jews to return to their capital.

332BC Jerusalem falls to Alexander the Great. After his death it passes to the Ptolemies of Egypt and later to the Seleucids of Syria, whose tyranny leads to the Maccabean revolt.

63BC Pompey takes the city for Rome.

70AD The major part of Jerusalem is destroyed by Titus.

135AD Following the second Jewish revolt the destruction commenced by Titus is completed and a new Roman city– Aelia Capitolina–is built on the site.

313AD Emperor Constantine proclaims the freedom and recognition of Christianity and, together with his mother, Helena, converts Jerusalem into a Christian city and restores its ancient name.

614AD The city is destroyed by the Persians.

637AD The Arabs occupy Jerusalem.

1009AD The Fatimite Caliphs destroy the Christian holy places.

1099AD The city is taken by the Crusaders under Godfrey de Bouillon.

1187AD After much internal quarrelling, the Crusaders are driven out by Saladin.

1517AD The city comes under Turkish domination.

1917AD Jerusalem surrenders to British troops under General Allenby.

Since 1948, when the British Mandate ran out, there have been periods of very uneasy peace broken by sudden outbreaks of bitter fighting. The effect of this on Jerusalem, ignoring the political implications and the rights or wrongs done by or to the various parties, has at least meant that one good has come out of it all, and that is that the city is no longer physically divided.

෴ ෴ ෴ ෴ ෴

As the rock over which the Dome of the Rock is built was once the holiest of holy places to the Jews, so the Church of the Holy Sepulchre is, without doubt, the centre of Christian faith and belief. I have always felt, watching pilgrims or visitors arriving in the forecourt before entering the church itself, that I would like to rush up and ask them, if it was their first visit, just what they were expecting to find, and again, when they left, if their expectations had been fulfilled. The fact is that this, in parts, ancient and venerable church satisfies no-one. It contains great beauty, and it also contains great ugliness. It might be supposed that as all the various religious bodies involved throughout its history in the building and restoration of this holy place shared a common faith they might at least have carried out their work with a common purpose, but this has been very far from the reality of the situation. There is hardly a square foot of space that has not been viciously fought over, time and time again, by the various divided sects within the Christian faith. It seems, sadly, that the blood that was once shed here for man's salvation has simply been added to a thousandfold by internal struggles to lay claim, exclusively, to small parts of the whole. Quite apart from squabbles of this kind, however, there is the bitter argument as to whether the building does, in fact, mark the actual site of the crucifixion and subsequent entombment. Being objective about it, it would be reasonable to say that it truly matters little whether this was the actual site or not, that it is the fact of the happening and the faith it gave rise to that are of much greater importance than the actual piece of ground on which it happened. This,, however, would be to deny man's determination to know these things for certain and, sometimes, to make the finding of an exact site of almost as much importance as the event itself. It is also true that there is a fascination to be found in standing in the exact spot where some great event took place; it is rather as though, standing there, we become almost a part of the event rather than mere onlookers–nonsense, as we all know–but it is a feeling we all get at some time in our lives.

The case for the authenticity of the site now commemorated as Calvary and the Tomb of Christ seems a pretty strong one, supported by a great deal of archaeological work. The Church of the Holy Sepulchre stands outside what were the city walls at the time of the crucifixion; of that there seems little doubt. The bulk of the evidence, however, is not archaeological but circumstantial, reinforced by strong reasoning. The romans were certainly not fools and it was only in 135 AD that the Emperor Hadrian decided to desecrate the principal shrine of the new religion that had emerged by building over it a pagan temple. It seems beyond the bounds of reason that he would have chosen, after such a short time and with so many people knowing the actual site, the wrong place in which to erect his desecratory shrine. If, therefore, we can accept the correct siting of this first building, then the rest follows almost automatically for, in 326 AD, the Emperor Constantine's mother arrived in Jerusalem and she was told, by various officials, what was common knowledge amongst the people; that beneath the pagan temple lay Calvary and the Tomb, the ground having been merely raised by infilling to provide the platform on which it was built. In effect, the Romans had been content to cover the site without destroying it and had thus preserved it almost intact. After clearing away the temple Constantine's chuch was built over and around Calvary and the Tomb. Despite being destroyed many times since, the church has always been rebuilt in the same place and evidence of all the earlier buildings still exists today.

Anyone entering the Church of the Holy Sepluchre without knowing anything of its history would almost certainly be a little bewildered. Except for two very old sets of stone steps leading to the Chapel of Golgotha, which rests, in part, on the summit of Calvary there is nothing to connect the maze of passages twisting all around the building and the smoke blackened walls and ceilings with a rocky hill outside the city walls and a nearby tomb in a garden. To be fair, it would be very surprising if such an important site did exist in anything like its original form, particularly when we realise that churches have been built over the holy places since the fourth century. When Constantine erected his original church most of the rock was cut away from around the tomb where Jesus was laid, leaving it isolated from its surroundings. It now has the appearance of a rather over ornate, heavily decorated shrine that has been built, rather than being the last surviving remnant of living rock out of which was carved the tomb. The same is true, to a great extent, of the rock of Calvary. This too has been cut away in places but at least it is possible to go under the Chapel of Golgotha and to see the original rock on which it rests.

Custody of, and responsibility for, the Church of the Holy Sepulchre is shared in varying proportions between no less than six different Christian sects; Roman Catholics, Greek Orthodox, Syrians, Armenians, Abbysinians and Copts and because of the intense rivalry, reaching bitterness that has in the past resulted in bloodshed between them it has, until recently, been virtually impossible to consider any major restorative work on the church. The rift between the sects is too deep and too old to expect any real degree of reconciliation to come about and it is very hard not to feel a sense of hopelessness and futility because of it. If all these holy men, united in the name of Christianity, cannot even agree about access to and restoration of their holiest shrine then the outlook for peace between the rest of us seems pretty remote.

On the credit side it must be said that, after so many years of virtual stagnation, the Church of the Holy Sepulchre is slowly being brought back to life. Nothing, of course, can be done about many of the less attractive additions to the church that have been forced upon it by misguided architects and builders in past years. At least work is now going on, however, to put right some of the damage that has been caused by the passing of time. Corrugated iron sheeting, blocks of stone, scaffolding and workmen hammering away at chisels may not be conducive to quiet meditation or, in my particular case to photography, but it nevertheless means that something is being done –only just in time. Already the scaffolding that disfigured the main entrance for so many years, (necessary, however, as the church was badly shaken and cracked during the earthquake of 1927), has now gone and the interior is starting to show the promise of what will be when the restoration work is finally completed.

☖ ☖ ☖ ☖ ☖

The Dome of the Rock dominates the city of Jerusalem. It would be reasonable to argue, and indeed it often is, that the site occupied by the Dome should be the principal Jewish place of worship. This was, after all, the situation that existed from the very beginning on Mount Moriah. The Jews, however, feeling perhaps that the destruction of the original Temple and the re-dedication of the site to other faiths throughout Jerusalem's history has brought about a barrier between themselves and the purity of worship they would wish, now venerate and worship at the oldest, most original part of the old Temple structure that still exists; the Wailing Wall. Wailing always seems to me an unfortunate choice of name for such a place. It conjures up entirely the wrong feeling, particularly to Western ears, and I would have thought Sorrowing would have described the Jewish people's feelings more accurately. Sorrow for the ideal that was lost, for the destruction of the Temple and for the years spent in exile.

After the Roman city of Aelia Capitolina was built over the destroyed Jerusalem it was decreed that the Jews would not be allowed to enter the new city. They were, however, allowed access to the sacred rock, to lament over their plight. This changed when the Rock was covered by the Muslim Dome and the Jews were left only with the Western Wall of Herod's Temple, left intact by Titus, as their sole surviving link with the glory of the Temple that once had been. Over the following centuries this fragment of the Temple became a symbol to Jews all over the world and they thought of it with longing, almost as though it was the Temple itself. There was even an attempt, in 1929, to turn the area of the Wall into a Synagogue but this idea was thwarted by an International Commission which decided that the Wall was Moslem property, although the Jews should have the right to pray there. After the 1967 war it was hardly surprising that the Jewish people would make their first priority the re-establishment of the Western Wall as their principal place of worship. The many houses and other buildings that had grown up near the Wall were removed and a wide, open space now leads up to the massive structure of the Wall itself. According to Jewish tradition, the sexes are segregated, the larger section, to the left, being reserved for the men and the right hand section for the women. It is to this place that Jews now come in their thousands to offer prayers, to ask for help needed, to give thanks for help received and, of course, to sorrow over all that once was.

As I left Jerusalem again I found my mind filled with pictures of all these people; Jewish, Christian and Moslem, concentrating so much thought and energy on their worship of one God and yet all striving to retain, at all costs, the differences between them that have been at the root of all their problems. There is no doubt that Jerusalem is quite unique in the way that it brings together three of the world's great religions and yet lets us see how daunting is the task of trying to ensure that different people, with differing beliefs, can eventually live side by side in harmony with each other.

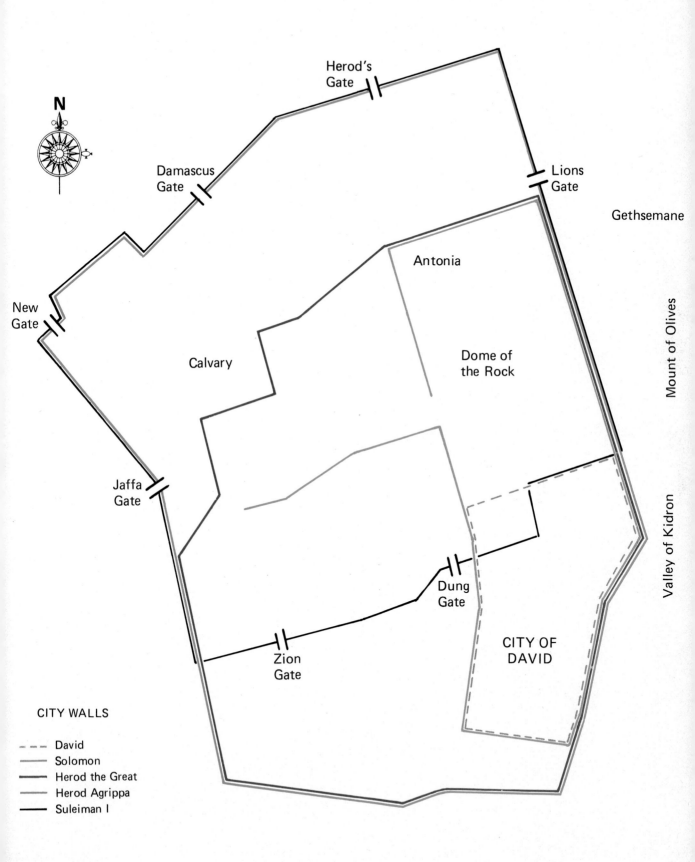

Herod's
Gate

N

Damascus
Gate

Lions
Gate

Gethsemane

New
Gate

Antonia

Mount of Olives

Calvary

Dome of
the Rock

Jaffa
Gate

Valley of Kidron

Dung
Gate

CITY OF
DAVID

Zion
Gate

CITY WALLS

- - - - David
——— Solomon
——— Herod the Great
——— Herod Agrippa
——— Suleiman I

The path leading from the foot of the Mount of Olives to the summit passes behind the Gethsemane Church of All Nations *right* and up, beyond the cupolas of the Russian church of Mary Magdalene. It is a steep twisting path and climbing it can be hot and tiring. Affording a welcome respite is the church of Dominus Flevit–The Lord Wept– where tradition tells us that Jesus wept over the city of Jerusalem. From the gardens *left* the city may be seen, shimmering in the hot sun. Stepping into the cool of the church itself provides a unique sight; Jerusalem seen across the altar and framed by the wrought-iron window *below* of the church. In the gardens of the church was discovered, in 1953, a necropolis of the Jewish and Byzantine period and it is possible to see some of the tombs and sarcophagi.

At the foot of the Mount of Olives stands the Gethsemane Church of All Nations *right* with its beautiful facade and statues of the four Evangelists.

The small and almost insignificant entrance *left* over which a mass of bouganvillea blossom cascades, is in marked contrast to the imposing and beautiful facade of the Gethsemane Church of All Nations– shown in more detail on the previous page. Outside the door the souvenir sellers wait with their offers, to the many visitors who come to the garden and church every day, of colour slides, film, postcards, trinkets and, of course, objects made, so the vendors always insist, of wood from the olive trees on the Mount of Olives, or even from the Garden of Gethsemane! If all the vendors of such objects were to be believed, then the Mount of Olives would be a barren place indeed, with not a tree to be seen! In fact, the contents of the garden, the flowers, the trees and, most of all the stones from the olives, are jealously guarded by the Fransiscans. They collect the olive stones and fashion them into rosaries, both for their own use and, occasionally, to be presented to visitors. Beyond the entrance lies the garden and through the garden a side door leads into the church itself.

It has been suggested that the olive trees in the Garden of Gethsemane *right* may be over two thousand years old. It is also understood, however, that all the trees in and around Jerusalem were felled by the soldiers of Titus in 70AD to be used in the building of his war machines. It would seem unlikely, therefore, that only these particular olive trees were spared. But it must also be said that, according to Pliny, "The olive tree never dies", and it may be that the present trees, even if not the contemporaries of Jesus, are shoots from the trees that existed at that time. Whatever the truth of their age, the trees are certainly very ancient and the Garden of Gethsemane–and its trees–hold a very special place in the hearts of most Christians.

From the earliest days of the Christian Church the site of the agony in the garden was greatly revered and, in the 4th century–in the time of Theodosius–a basilica was erected there. It was subsequently destroyed by the Persians, rebuilt by the Crusaders and then destroyed yet again. The site was excavated in 1891 and plans were made to erect a new church. The present basilica *above* was finished by the Franciscans in 1924 and, as many different peoples throughout the world had helped to finance its building, the coats of arms of the United States, Canada, Germany, Great Britain, Belgium, Spain, France, Italy, Chile, Mexico, Brazil, Argentina, Poland, Eire, Hungary and Australia are all incorporated in the mosaics and the iron grill; hence the name–Church of All Nations.

Alabaster windows, which are translucent, allow a dim, purple light to filter through and illuminate the interior in the most restful way–entirely in keeping with the purpose of the church. Six columns support the twelve cupolas which form the body of the church and this gives the impression of prostration before the rock of the Agony which rises through the floor.

Above and to the right of the Church of All Nations is the beautiful and distinctive Russian church of Mary Magdalene, built in 1888 by Czar Alexander III in memory of his mother, the Empress Maria Alexandrovna. In the grounds of the Russian church are the remains of the ancient road that led to the summit of the Mount of Olives.

When we think of Jerusalem we instinctively connect it, in our minds, with its place in the history of three of the world's great religions and, of course, this is understandable. It would be wrong, however, to assume that this is all there is to Jerusalem; that it is merely a museum or a religious centre and nothing more. Jerusalem, both without and within the city walls, is a lively, bustling city. Within the old city there are certainly no department stores or large shops but it is, nevertheless, a very alive and vital place. Quite apart from the many visitors from all over the world, the parties of tourists being conducted from or to this or that place of interest, the narrow streets are thronged with people going about their business; housewives buying provisions for their families, deliveries being made–often by donkey–and Arabs from outlying areas selling their small amount of home-grown produce by the roadside. The souvenir shops, of course, are everywhere; it is difficult to walk more than a few yards down any of the streets without coming across yet another. As with most cities where tourism plays a large part in the economy there is good and bad to be found; shops that sell cheap, tasteless rubbish and others that have exquisite workmanship on show. There are 'guides' who will extract the most they can from gullible tourists and show them around the holy places with a complete disregard for the truth, and

there are others who are knowledge-able, courteous and fair.

The great majority of the streets in the old city are far too narrow and crowded to allow the entry of motor vehicles and, as the city is built on two hills, the streets are often steep and, indeed, stepped. The ability and apparent willingness of donkeys to carry such a heavy burden, plus a rider, is a source of amazement to many visitiors to Jerusalem. Donkeys are to be seen everywhere, carrying anything from rubble, where building is in progress, to containers of kerosene or milk. When donkeys are not being used porters carry enormous loads on their backs or, like the one below, use peculiar three-wheeled barrows, reminiscent of the old ice cream carts, which, particularly when in the charge of the youngsters, are often to be seen hurtling down hills with their 'drivers' sliding along behind them in a desperate and for the most part successful effort to control them.

It is difficult to imagine a building more beautiful than the Dome of the Rock, pictured on these and the following pages. It stands on the summit of Mount Moriah–so called in memory of Abraham's sacrifice. A temple was originally built by Solomon on the site but it was not until the 7th century that it started to take anything like its present form. Successively restored, it achieved the height of its magnificence under Suleiman the Magnificent in the 16th century, and it was at this time that the outer part was covered with coloured tiles, details of which are shown overleaf.

Under the Dome, and surrounded by the iron screen of the Crusaders, lies the rock, made sacred by history and legend. Here Abraham was prepared to sacrifice his son Isaac and it was this rock that became the foundation of the holocaust altar. According to the Muslims, Mohammed came to Jerusalem and prayed on the rock before continuing his journey to heaven on his magnificent steed Burak, a gift from the Archangel Gabriel.

In the time of Herod the Great a magnificent Temple was built on the site of the old; on the summit of Mount Moriah. All that remains of this building, apart from the Rock itself, is the western, or wailing wall. Following the Arab conquest of Jerusalem in 638AD a building was erected over the Rock but the Dome of the Rock as we know it was not completed until 691.

Mohammed did not see himself as a Messiah but, rather, as the last of the great line of prophets, many of whom are common to the Koran and the Old and New Testaments. Abraham, therefore, occupies a place of importance to the Muslims that corresponds to that afforded him by the Jews–and, indeed, the Christians. Because of this the Rock on Mount Moriah has a special significance to the followers of Mohammed, not only as Abraham's sacrificial altar, but also as the place made holy by the Prophet when he stopped to pray there on his journey to visit the other prophets in heaven. According to the religion of Islam the Rock is the foundation stone of the world, exceeded in holiness only by the Kaaba stone in Mecca.

The first Muslim construction over the Rock was a wooden mosque, but this was only a temporary expedient, to be superseded by the Dome of the Rock proper, which was built between 687 and 791 by the Caliph Abd al-Malik, who used for the purpose a great number of Roman pillars and stones as well as employing architects and designers local to the area. The use of pillars from other buildings accounts for the difference in styles that are apparent today.

In 1099 the Crusaders transformed the mosque into a Christian sanctuary, giving it the name *Templum Domini* and handed it over to the custody of a Chapter of the Canons of St. Augustine. This was not to last for long, however, and in 1187, when Jerusalem was recaptured by Saladin, the golden cross on the top of the dome was removed–to be replaced by the Crescent of Islam.

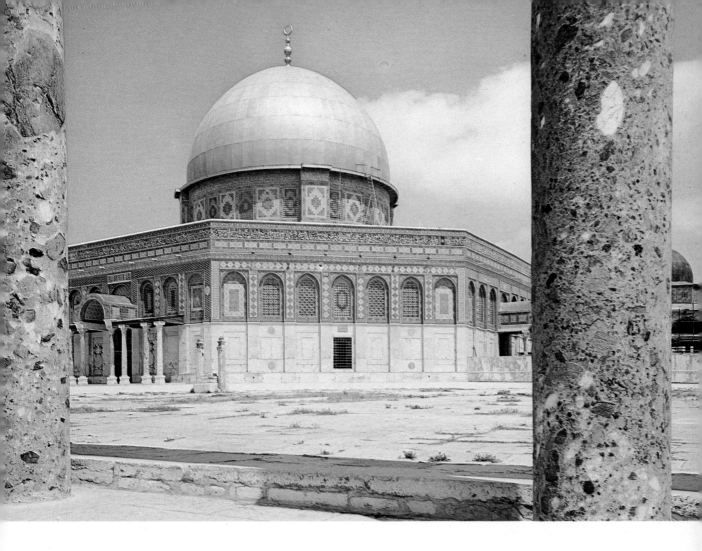

Framed between two massive pillars stands the Dome of the Rock *above* in splendid isolation on the summit of Mount Moriah. The pillars support arches, called *Mawazin*–which means 'scales'–by the Muslims, as they believe that from these arches scales will be suspended, to be used in the weighing of souls on the day of judgement.

The exquisite building, a perfect octagon, is crowned by the dome, sheathed in gold-plated aluminium. Although this may not match the richness of the original dome, which legend tells us was covered with solid gold, the present structure at least matches the original in appearance, and is a vast improvement on the dull, lead dome that was erected in the 11th century.

After the narrow, crowded and sometimes evil-smelling streets of the old city, the vast, open space in which the Dome of the Rock stands is almost like a breath of fresh air, and the very contrast makes the peace and quiet of this holy place seem even more unreal.

A niche in the wall inside the Dome of the Rock indicates to the true follower of Mohammed the direction of Mecca, towards which he will face during his daily prayers.

Eight wide flights of steps lead up to the platform on which the Dome of the Rock stands–and which is the summit of Mount Moriah. The whole effect is one of immense spaciousness. The soaring arches *left* span elegant pillars, many of them bound with iron hoops now to add support to them because of their great age.

Fed by the waters of Solomon's aqueduct is El Kas, *below* the ablution fountain at which the Muslim faithful carry out the obligatory washing of hands, feet and head before entering the mosque to pray.

At the southern end of the esplanade stands the El Aqsa Mosque *right*–the distant mosque–so called because at the time that it was built, at the beginning of the 8th century, it was the most distant mosque from Mecca. Although it does not, perhaps, have the unique splendour of the nearby Dome of the Rock, the El Aqsa Mosque is a fascinating building in its own right. Parts of the original structure still survive to the present day as part of the extensive renovation and rebuilding that took place between 1938 and 1942.

All over Jerusalem constant excavation and reconstruction *above* is carried out and the results of this work are to be seen almost everywhere.

The Temple Area, or Haram Esh-Sharif, contains a wealth of sanctuaries, shrines and memorials, *left* the names of which have often been changed over the centuries to fit in with the ideas and beliefs of the city's many conquerors.

The interior of the El Aqsa Mosque *right* reveals an impressive open space of approximately 85 metres long by 60 metres wide. Much of the material used in its construction was taken from St. Mary's Church and this lends to the building a peculiar church-like feeling. The whole of the floor is covered with large carpet squares in a variety of patterns. The priceless pulpit, constructed in Aleppo without the use of nails, and the gift of Saladin, was sadly destroyed in 1969 by an arsonist who managed to gain entry to the mosque with a can of kerosene, with the result that an irreplaceable work of art was lost to the world.

Small boys selling their wares from a bench in the old city *above* are suddenly aware of the camera and unsure whether they want to be photographed or not.

Two time-honoured methods of carrying loads. A heavily laden donkey *left* and two equally heavily laden women *right* and always in evidence, the ubiquitous plastic shopping bag.

It is possible to buy an enormous variety of goods in the old city, from exotic souvenirs to simple, everyday fresh fruit and vegetables *below*.

It is difficult to imagine that the assortment of towers and cupolas *overleaf* in reality mark the site of a hill and a garden tomb, but such is the case with the Church of the Holy Sepulchre.

A small arched doorway *left* provides access to the courtyard *right* of the group of chapels, churches and monasteries that, together, make up the Church of the Holy Sepulchre. The door at the right has been bricked up since the time of Saladin.

From the inside of the church, looking towards the main entrance *below*. The Stone of the Anointing is at the bottom left of the picture, surrounded by eight candelabra.

The Roman Catholic altar *far right top* on the summit of the rock of Calvary, dates from the latter part of the 16th century.

The Church of the Holy Sepulchre takes its name from the tomb *far right bottom* where the body of Jesus was laid after the crucifixion. Most of the rock from which the tomb was carved has been cut away and what remains has been richly panelled, pillared and decorated *bottom right* by the various Christian sects into whose care it is entrusted.

Bethlehem, the birthplace of King David and of Jesus, lies about eleven miles south of Jerusalem. The present Church of the Nativity dates from the 6th century and, because the Magi were depicted as Persians in the mosaics, it is said to be the only church they spared when they over-ran the country in 614AD.

Christmas bells *left* still hung with coloured electric lights, above the Church of the Nativity.

The main entrance to the Church of the Nativity *below* has a doorway so small that it is necessary to bend almost double to gain access.

The focal point of the church in Bethlehem is the silver star *right* which marks the place of the Nativity. This particular star dates from 1717 and the Latin inscription around it reads–Hic de Virgine Maria Jesus Christus natus est'– (Here was Jesus Christ born of the Virgin Mary).

David's Citadel and the Tower of David *above and left* stand close to the Jaffa Gate and form part of the west wall of the city. A great deal of archaeological excavation is being carried out here, particularly at the base of the massive city walls.

The monument known as Absalom's Pillar *right* in the Valley of Kidron with, beyond it, the east wall of the city, culminating in the pinnacle of the Temple at the left.

David's third son, Absalom, exploited anything that could bring about discontent in the tribes. He eventually had himself proclaimed king, and this inevitably meant that a battle was fought between the forces of David and those of Absalom. In the battle Absalom was defeated, and in attempting to escape, legend has it that his long hair caught in the low branches of a tree, from which he was suspended helplessly until the arrival of David's forces, who killed him.

Although the pillar commemorates Absalom it is distinctly Hellenic in style and it was probably the tomb of a wealthy Greek family.

The Israel Museum complex, with the coolly welcoming sound of its waterfalls and the landscaped beauty of its sculpture gardens, provides a fitting showcase for a large number of treasured and fascinating exhibits. High on the list of anyone interested in a study of the Holy Land must be the Dead Sea Scrolls, housed in the Shrine of the Book, *right*, designed to represent, from the outside, the lid of one of the earthenware jars in which the scrolls were discovered, in a remote cave by the Dead Sea.

South from the Jaffa Gate lies Yemin Moshe. A settlement dating from the latter half of the nineteenth century, it was the result of a dream of a new Jerusalem outside the walls of the old city. Standing somewhat incongruously atop the old settlement and dwarfed, now, by the encroaching high rise blocks stands the Montefiore Windmill, *left*, named after Sir Moses Montefiore whose vision and idealism brought about the building of Yemin Moshe which was to lead, eventually, to the construction of the modern Jerusalem we see today.

Sightless eyes and a grotesquely twisted nose in the side of a hillock opposite the Damascus Gate bear an uncanny resemblance to a skull, *left.* The site excited General Gordon of Khartoum, a devout Christian, sufficiently for him to make an exhaustive search of the adjacent area. The eventual discovery, nearby, of an ancient oil press and a tomb cut out of the solid rock convinced him that he had found the true site of Calvary, or Golgotha–the place of the skull. Authentic or not, the whole site is now preserved, with its relics, in the form of a very beautiful and peaceful garden which certainly gives some idea of how the area now covered by the Church of the Holy Sepulchre must have looked two thousand years ago.

Grouped amongst trees, a short distance west of the old city, stand the Convention Centre, the Hebrew University, the Planetarium, the Stadium and the Israel Museum, from which may be seen the uncompromising squareness of the Knesset, *right,* Israel's new Parliament building with its superb Chagall hall.

An Israeli soldier *left* sits on the wall directly above the busy Damascus Gate, one of the main entrances into the old city, keeping a watchful eye on the comings and goings below him. The walls and the city's narrow, twisting streets are regularly patrolled by troops, but the city has seen it all before; it seems that there have always been troops of one power or another in Jerusalem throughout its long and troubled history.

Most of the streets in the old city are very narrow *below, far left* and, with the awnings over the shops and stalls—or the buildings themselves—almost meeting overhead, only a narrow band of sunlight is allowed to filter through and illuminate the cobbles.

A small boy, probably unaware that he is surrounded by so much history sees only an inquisitive photographer and, equally inquisitive himself, obliges him with a backwards glance.

Carrying his wares strapped firmly on his back and around his waist, a tea vendor *above* dispenses hot, sweet tea to passers by. On a hot, dry day there are few drinks more refreshing than his. The decorated and polished urn on his back contains the tea and the spout sticks out from under his left arm. In his left hand he carries a heavy brass water container to rinse out the glasses before they are returned to the tray at his waist.

Traders and craftsmen are to be found by the roadside throughout the streets of the old city. Some are relatively well equipped and others may only have an old box containing a few apples or some pieces of material and it is difficult to see how some of them manage to make any sort of living at all. Others, like the shoe seller pictured here *left* supplement their few sales by carrying out minor repairs with only the very minimum of equipment.

The colour and excitement of a ceremony at the wailing wall *overleaf* as relatives and friends shout encouragement and record the scene for family albums.

The earliest records refer to Jerusalem as Salem and, later, Urusalem –certainly one of the most important cities of Palestine–although subject to the power of Egypt. When David eventually took the city a palace was built on Mount Zion and defences were erected around the city.

When David was growing old, he had his son Solomon anointed king. At the same time he commanded Solomon to build a Temple on Mount Moriah, something David had been unable to accomplish in his own lifetime because he had been too occupied in wars and establishing the kingdom. After David died, Solomon approached Hiram, the king of Tyre, and asked him to build the Temple. Cedars were brought from the Lebanon to the port of Jaffa and then overland to by used in the Temple's construction. The top of Mount Moriah, where Abraham had prepared to sacrifice his son Isaac, was levelled and on it was built the Temple, together with a royal palace and a mound to connect the new buildings with the city of David, and around it all he built a wall, known as the first wall.

In the 6th century BC Nebuchadnezzar laid siege to the city, destroyed the Temple and led the people away into captivity. Under the edict of Cyrus the Jews were permitted to return to Jerusalem, and they did so, restoring the altar and the Temple, but this state of affairs only lasted until the domination of Israel by Persia, followed by the conquest by Alexander the Great in 331BC. After the break-up of Alexander's empire Jerusalem passed into the hands of the Ptolemies of Egypt, and later the Seleucids of Syria. The tyranny of Antiochus was directly responsible for the rise of the Maccabees, a rise to power that restored some of the greatness that had been Jerusalem's during the reign of Solomon. Once again, however, the problem of internal discord arose in the city and, this time, it led to the intervention of the greatest power the world had known; the power of Rome. Pompey made himself master of Jerusalem in 63BC and in 37BC the Romans installed Herod as king; an act that was to have far-reaching consequences so far as the Jerusalem we know today is concerned.

The many magnificent buildings that were commenced during the reign of Herod the Great were, alas, destroyed by the soldiers of Titus in 70AD. There was one notable exception, however, and that was the western wall of Herod's Temple, which was left virtually intact. It is believed that this was done deliberately to show the world the might of Rome and to act as an object lesson to all; to show that even buildings of a magnitude such as this had fallen before Rome's power. It is this wall that is the subject of these pages; a wall constructed of huge limestone blocks and which reaches a height of almost sixty feet, dwarfing the figures of the people who come here to pray.

After the destruction of the old city of Jerusalem by Titus in 70AD the Romans built on the site a new city, Aelia Capitolina, in 135AD. The Jews were not allowed to enter the new city but they were permitted to weep on the sacred rock that had been the holocaust altar of their Temple.

When Jerusalem fell to the Arabs the rock was covered by the Dome of the Rock and so even this holy place was denied to the Jews. They had to be content with coming to the wall, the only remaining part of their original Temple and there they sorrowed, not least for all that had been and was now no more.

There have been attempts in the past to build a synagogue at the wall and in 1929 this idea caused a great deal of trouble. Eventually, after an International Commission, the idea was abandoned. Today there are other plans, one of which is to excavate the wall to an even lower level, to go even further back in history to a time nearer to the origins of the Temple, and impressions of some of these ideas are on view in the musuem by the Jaffa Gate.

Whatever may happen in the future, the wall is a place of the utmost sanctity to Jews from all over the world, many thousands of whom travel great distances to visit and pray at this venerable place. At sunset each day, but particularly on holy days, Jews arrive from all parts of the city and, indeed, from much further afield to offer their prayers and, sometimes, to push written requests into the spaces between the great stones, there, they hope, to find a more direct route to God.

Some idea of the part of the wall that is at present above the ground may be gained from this view *above*. At the wall the men are segregated from the women by a fence. Beyond and above the wall rises the huge dome of the Dome of the Rock, under which is the sacred holocaust altar of Solomon's Temple.

On the summit of the Mount of Olives stands the now rather forlorn-looking Chapel of the Ascension *above*. A Crusaders reconstruction, it stands on the site of the original church built in 378AD. In 1187 the place was converted into a mosque and the arcades of the edicule were walled up.

Stones on the tombs in the Jewish cemetery *left* are left by visitors to commemorate their attendance. The sinking sun brilliantly backlights the Dome of the Rock in the middle distance and some of the newer towers on the skyline.